Sacred Spirit

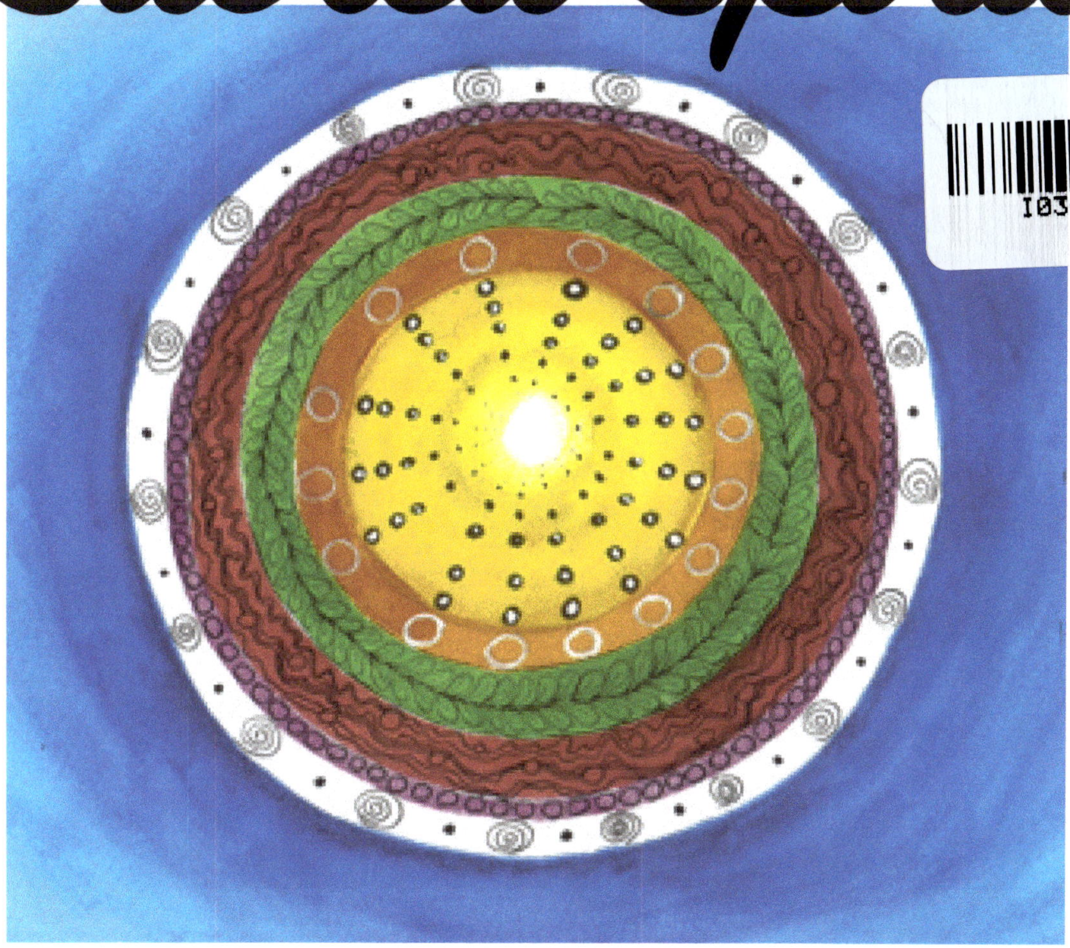

THE GRAND ORIGINAL DESIGN

Gemma Schooneveldt

First published in Australia in 2021
by Gemma Schooneveldt
e-mail: gemmani@iprimus.com.au
in conjunction with Spectrum Publications Pty Ltd
www.spectrumpublications.com.au

Copyright 2021
All rights reserved.
No part of this publication may be reproduced
in any manner without prior
written permission of the publisher.

Artwork by Gemma Schooneveldt
and her grandson, Lawson.

ISBN 978-0-867860481

Some suggestions for using this book:
An adult could read to a young child?
What is your favourite page?

Is there a question you would like to ask?
Draw your own picture?
Make up a song?

Long, long ago,
before the world was as we
know it today,
before the Common Era, known as BCE,
there was ………

Some people call GOD:
Good Orderly Direction

or

The Creator

or

A Higher Power

or

The Universe

or

The Grand Original Design

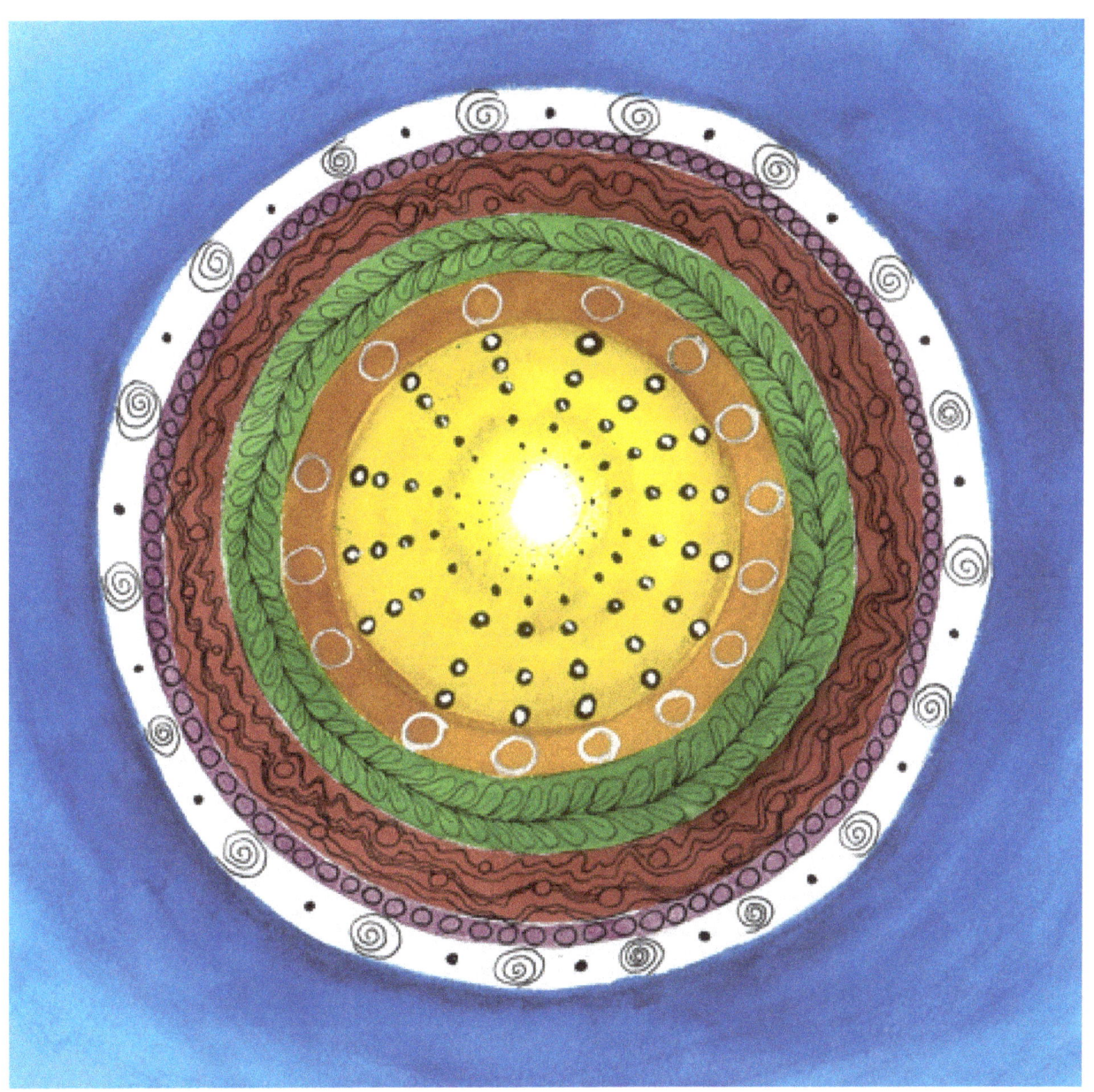

GOD loved this world
and saw
that it was good.

The people in this world
were good too.
But some started to fight
with each other
and take things
that didn't belong to them.

They forgot to be grateful
for all
they had been given
by GOD.

GOD
looked at all this fighting
and wondered
how people could get to know
GOD
and know each other
and become peaceful again.

So GOD decided to
send us a human being,
Jesus,
to live amongst the people
and show us new ways
of living,
sharing
and loving.

Jesus was born
more than 2000 years ago.

There are many stories
about him
in an amazing book called
The Bible.

Many people followed Jesus' way
and just before he died,
he promised he would leave us
his Spirit -
to be with us always.

This Spirit lives inside us
and gives us
courage,
hope
and joy.

Jesus said to them,
It is I; I am with you;
do not be afraid.

(cf. Jn: 6:20)

Acknowledgements

The seeds of my little booklet were planted more than fifty years ago.
At that time, I was a young person who had some big struggles in my life.
But somehow God stayed with me and gave me courage to keep going.
I am so grateful to be part of a large family – siblings, children,
grand-children, in-laws and extensive family.
Special thanks go to my grandson Lawson, who was 10 years old when he drew these illustrations,
and to Rev Barry Moran, Jill McCorquodale and Dr Robyn Reynolds olsh,
for their support and encouragement.

This book is dedicated to my grandchildren:
Wil, Tehya, Lani, Aiden, Lawson, Gypsea and Sophie
… and to all seekers of truth.

Copyright © Gemma Schooneveldt 2020

www.ingramcontent.com/pod-product-compliance
Lightning Source LLC
Chambersburg PA
CBHW061818290426
44110CB00026B/2910